CHRIS VAN ALLSBURG

BAD DAY AT

RIVERBEND

To Sophia, My Little Buckaroo

HOUGHTON MIFFLIN COMPANY BOSTON

1 9 9 5

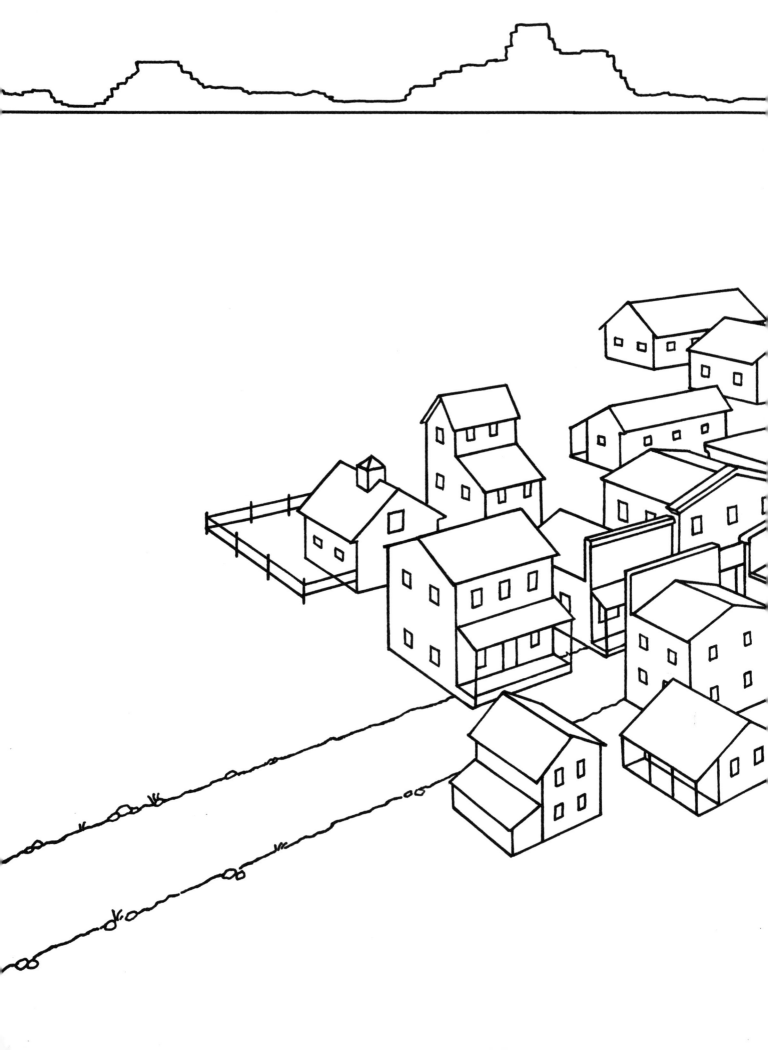

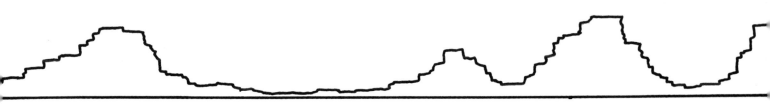

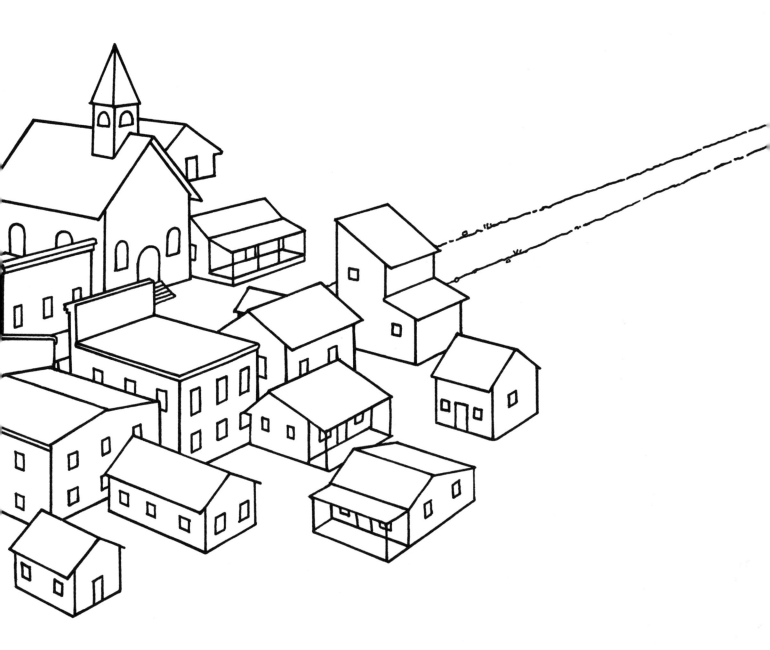

Riverbend was a quiet little town—just a couple dozen buildings alongside a dusty road that led nowhere. Though the stagecoach occasionally rolled through town, it never stopped because no one ever came to Riverbend and no one ever left. It was the kind of place where one day was just like all the rest.

But one morning Sheriff Ned Hardy stood in front of the Riverbend jail and saw something he'd never seen before. A brilliant light in the western sky. It lasted a few minutes, then faded away.

Sheriff Hardy went into the jailhouse. He was sitting quietly at his desk, wondering what the strange light meant, when a loud pounding rattled the jailhouse door.

The sheriff opened it and saw Owen Buck, the blacksmith's boy, breathing so hard he could barely speak. In between gasps, Ned Hardy heard the words "stagecoach" and "something awful."

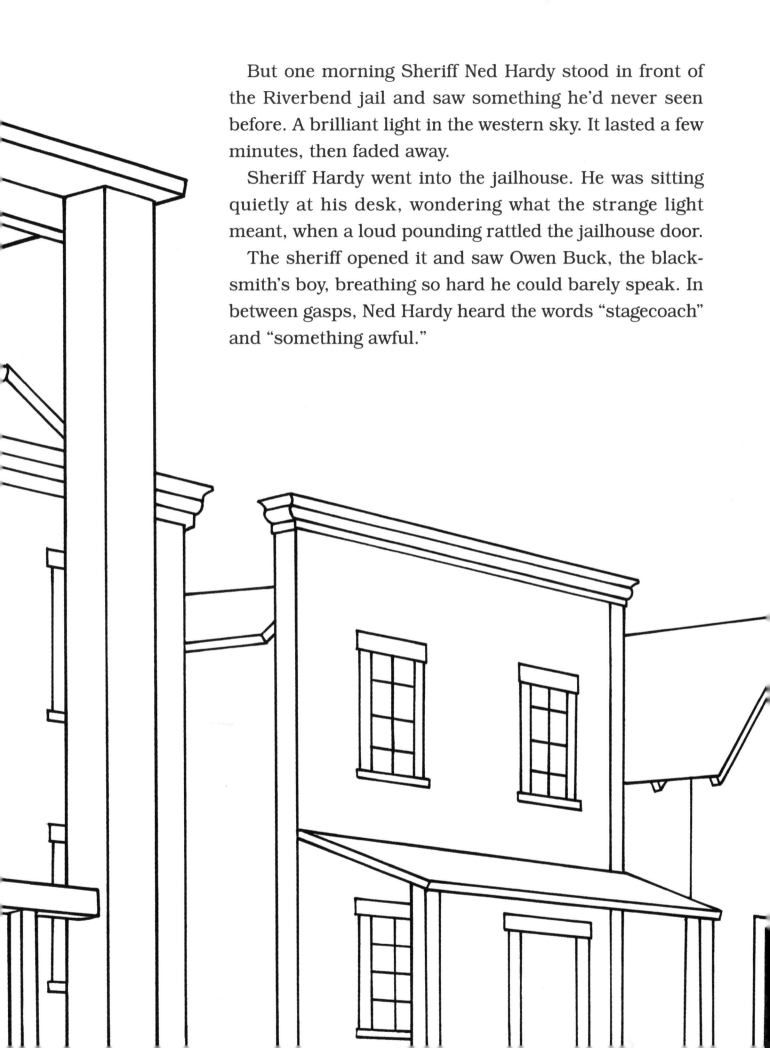

The sheriff followed Owen outside. The coach had never stopped in Riverbend before, but now it stood motionless at the end of the street. A crowd gathered around it, but they held back, as if they were afraid to get too close.

It was easy to see why. The horses were covered with great stripes of some kind of shiny, greasy slime.

"What is it, sheriff?" someone asked as Ned Hardy stepped up to the coach. He didn't know. It was the strangest thing he'd ever seen, the strangest thing anyone had ever seen.

The horses were nervous and breathing hard. They looked terrible, their smooth white coats scarred with the strange stuff that hung from them in loopy ropes or stuck out like stiff wire. The sheriff grabbed a piece with both hands. It was slippery. He gave it a pull, and the horse jerked away and whinnied in pain. Whatever the stuff was, it stuck to them as sure as their flesh.

"Where's the coachman?" Sheriff Hardy asked.

"Gone," someone answered. "The coach came into town without him."

Ned Hardy wasn't sure what to do. He scratched his head. "Well," he finally said. "Guess I'll go look for him."

The sheriff rode out of town, following the wagon's trail west. Before long he stopped his horse. The ground was covered with the same marks that were on the horses. Whatever happened must have happened here. He didn't see any sign of the driver, but he heard a muffled sound.

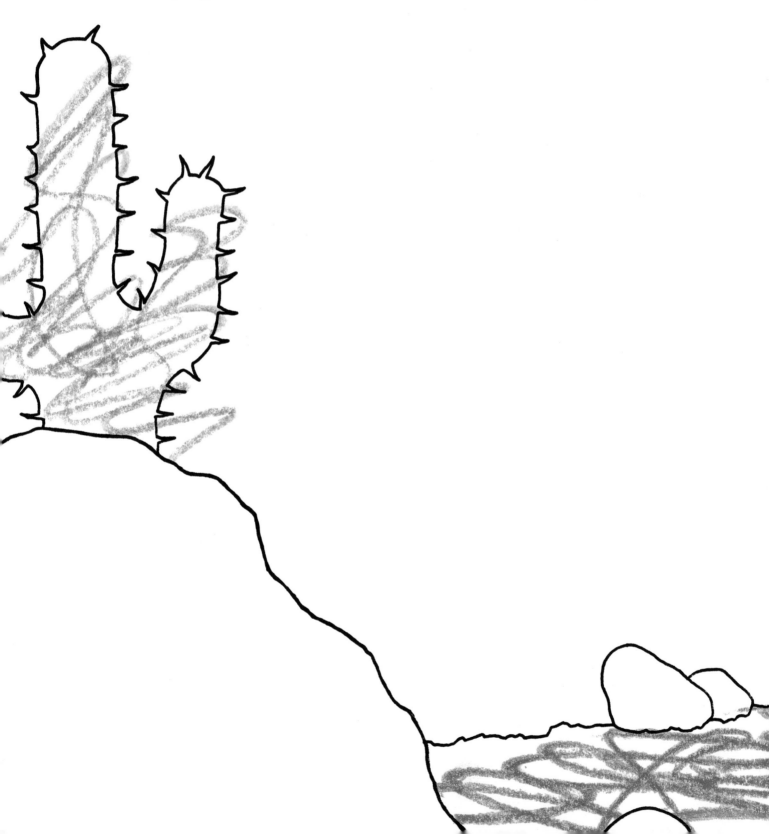

Ned Hardy got off his horse and discovered the coachman sitting on the ground behind a rock. The poor man looked awful. He was covered with the greasy slime. Thick stripes of the stuff ran right across his eyes and mouth. He couldn't see or speak, except to mumble.

The sheriff helped the coachman up and led him to the horse. As they rode together back toward Riverbend, Ned Hardy heard the sound of thundering hoofbeats. He rode to the top of the ridge and looked down on a charging herd of cattle, many marked with the awful slime that covered his poor saddlemate.

When he turned his horse back toward town, he saw the same bright light in the sky he'd seen that morning. It was just beyond the horizon, right over Riverbend. It didn't last long.

As he approached Riverbend, it was clear to Ned Hardy, even from a distance, that something terrible had happened. Riding into town, he could barely bring himself to look at the buildings, now covered with the hideous marks and stripes. The sheriff got out of the saddle. The town looked deserted, but when he passed the hotel, someone called out, "Sheriff." Ned Hardy helped the coach driver down and led him to the hotel.

The townspeople and some cowboys were gathered inside. A few were covered with the greasy slime. They all told the same story: Without warning, the sky overhead had filled with a brilliant light, a light that froze everything it touched—herds of cattle, even birds in the sky. And it was blinding.

"Like stepping out of a privy and looking straight into the sun at high noon," one of the cowboys said. "Couldn't see a darn thing." When the light passed, they were covered with the greasy marks.

"What are we gonna do, sheriff?" someone asked. "We can't spend our lives hiding in here."

"No," Ned Hardy said. "No we can't." He walked outside and stood in front of the hotel. His bravery inspired the others and they joined him there. They looked at their poor town. Pretty little Riverbend was now too ugly for words.

"Look," someone shouted, pointing at the sky above the hills just out of town.

The mysterious light appeared. Some people ran back inside the hotel, but Ned Hardy just stared at the strange light without blinking an eye.

"Whatever evil thing has done this is out in those hills," he said, pointing in the direction of the light. "I aim to ride out there and put an end to it."

The sheriff left town with a posse of well-armed men. They followed the trail of light. It wasn't hard to tell where it had been. The greasy streaks were everywhere. The men even saw them floating in the sky. But the light they sought always appeared just beyond the horizon.

Then they saw the mysterious light shine brightly just over the next hill. The men crawled up the hill, but the light faded away as they peeked over the top. Looking down, the brave cowboys saw something that made them gasp. There was a man standing perfectly still at the bottom of the hill. He was as tall as a cottonwood tree and as skinny as a broomstick. And he looked like he was made entirely of the greasy stuff that now covered the countryside.

Ned Hardy was sure that this long-legged fellow was the cause of all their grief. They had only one chance. They'd have to get close enough to take a shot at this skinny devil before he used the light to freeze them. They crawled back to their horses. Ned Hardy gave a silent signal and the posse charged forward.

But just as they came over the hill, they were frozen in the bright light that suddenly filled the sky.

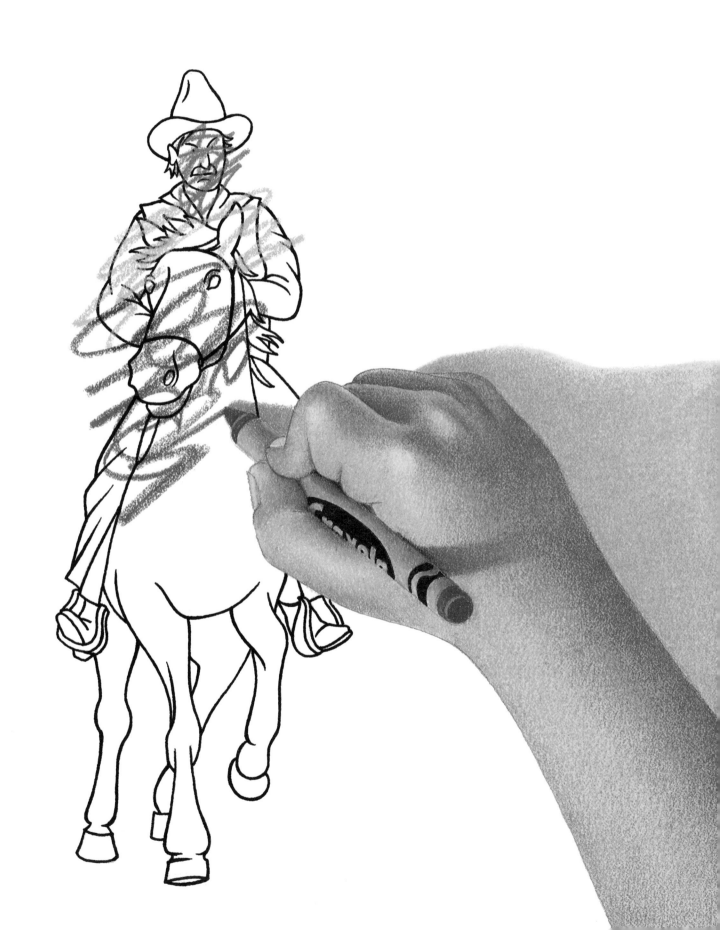

And then the light went out.